NATIONAL GEOGRAPHIC

T0045064

Ladders

Mountains, Valleys, and Plains

EARTH LAND

by Richard Easby

From high above Earth, you can see our planet's amazing features. There are high **mountains** with snow-covered peaks. They can be cold, windy places where few plants and animals survive. In other areas deep, wide **valleys** snake across the land. Rivers run along the bottom of many valleys. You can also see flat **plains** stretching to the horizon. Let's get to know some of these wonderful **landforms.**

Hudson Bay

GREAT PLAINS

Mississippi R.

APPALACHIAN MT

PACIFIC OCEAN

Caribb

Rocky Mountains

A mountain is a very high place with steep sides.

The Rocky Mountains stretch between the United States and Canada. Some of its peaks are over 4,267 meters (14,000 feet) high.

...S

...ORMS

Indus Valley

A valley is a low land bordered by higher land.

The Indus Valley is in Asia. The valley was shaped by the Indus River. It stretches nearly 3,000 kilometers (1,864 miles), across the countries of India and Pakistan, to the Arabian Sea. The valley is the site of some of Earth's earliest civilizations.

North
Sea

RHINE RIVER VALLEY

A L P S

Danube R.   Black Sea

Mediterranean Sea

ATLAS MTS.

ZAGROS MTS.

Caspian
Sea

Euphrates R.

Tigris R.

HIMALAYA

Huang He
(Yellow R.)

NORTH
CHINA
PLAIN

Chang Jiang
(Yangtze R.)

Ganges R.

ATLANTIC
OCEAN

PACIFIC
OCEAN

Niger R.

Nile R.

GREAT
RIFT
VALLEY

Congo R.

Arabian
Sea

Bay of
Bengal

INDIAN OCEAN

Serengeti Plain

A plain is a large, flat area of land.

The Serengeti Plain stretches across the countries of Kenya and Tanzania in Africa. It is a large, flat grassland. Herds of zebras, elephants, lions, and other wildlife live on the plain.

Prepare yourself! You are about to explore three of the most interesting destinations on the planet. We'll start with the Andes Mountains, South America's longest mountain range. Next we'll travel to the Rhine River Valley, one of Europe's largest valleys. Finally we'll visit Asia's North China Plain, one of the most populated places on Earth. You'll discover how these landforms were shaped by nature. You will also learn what it's like to live in each place.

∨ North China Plain

4

ANDES MOUNTAINS

The Andes are high mountains with sharp, jagged peaks. The Andes stretch from Venezuela to Argentina. Ancient civilizations, including the Inca, once lived within the mountains.

Rhine Valley

The Rhine River formed the Rhine Valley. The river begins as a mountain stream in Switzerland. It travels through Germany, France, and the Netherlands, forming a wide valley.

North China Plain

The North China Plain is a vast, flat area. The plain is made of deep layers of sediments deposited by rivers. The plain is mostly used for farmland, but the city of Beijing is on its northern edge.

Check In   Compare and contrast mountains, valleys, and plains.

ANDES MOUNTAINS

by Christopher Siegel

HOLA Y BIENVENIDOS A LA CORDILLERA DE LOS ANDES!

Hello and welcome to the Andes Mountains!

Don't get dizzy because of the height! You are on top of some of the tallest **mountains** in the world. Some of the summits are almost 6,100 meters (20,000 feet) above sea level.

The Andes are also one of the longest groups of mountains in the world. The Andes stretch for about 7,000 kilometers (4,350 miles) over much of the continent of South America.

The rock on the mountain peaks is rough and jagged. Some mountains have sharp ridges that connect the peaks. Ice created many of these rocky formations through **weathering.** Water freezes in cracks in rock. The water expands as it turns to ice. This causes the rock to split apart, creating beautiful rocky mountain peaks.

The Andes are located in South America.

Water seeps into the cracks of rocks. When the water freezes, it expands. This causes the rock to break apart.

LIVING IN THE MOUNTAINS

CLIMATE

High in the Andes, the air is often cold and dry. The highest peaks have snow year round. The weather doesn't change much.

TRANSPORTATION

Mountains have steep slopes and the rock breaks apart and wears away. The loose rock can create dangerous mountain landslides.

WHERE PEOPLE LIVE

The Andes Mountains are rocky with very thin soil. The climate is cold. Grasses and some crops can grow in the Andes, but it is hard for trees to grow there.

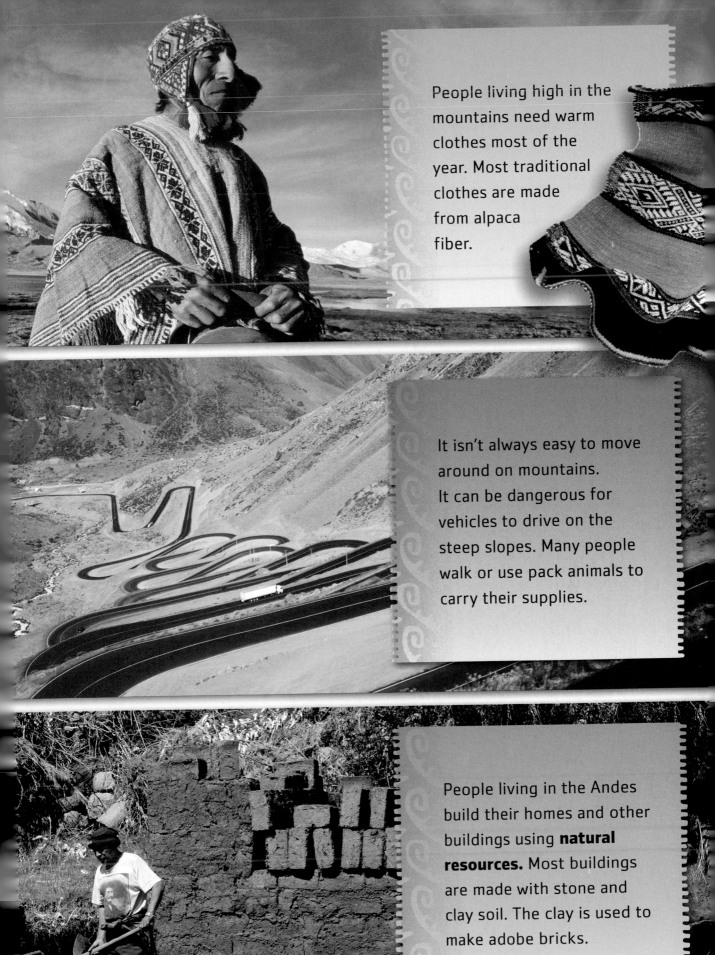

People living high in the mountains need warm clothes most of the year. Most traditional clothes are made from alpaca fiber.

It isn't always easy to move around on mountains. It can be dangerous for vehicles to drive on the steep slopes. Many people walk or use pack animals to carry their supplies.

People living in the Andes build their homes and other buildings using **natural resources.** Most buildings are made with stone and clay soil. The clay is used to make adobe bricks.

ALPACAS

The Andes are home to a herd animal called an alpaca. Ancient Incan civilization valued alpaca fleece, the animals' soft outer coat. It was called the "fiber of the gods." There are still herds of alpacas on the mountainous Andes landscape. People use the fleece to make hats, ponchos, blankets, and other woven items.

1. HERDING Alpacas are herd animals and generally stay together. Herds are watched over by their owners.

2. SHEARING
Alpacas are sheared at least once a year. The fleece is removed from the animal much like a haircut. The fleece eventually grows back.

3. DYEING
Alpaca fleece can be dyed into many colors. Many dyes are made from plants that grow in the Andes.

4. KNITTING AND WEAVING
Alpaca fiber is spun together into yarn. This yarn is knitted or woven into cloth and other fabrics. Many colorful items are made from it.

5. AT THE MARKET
Markets and shops in the Andes sell items made of alpaca fiber. The woven clothes are popular with local people and with tourists.

Check In   How are the Andes different from where you live?

Rhine Valley

by Lara Winegar

Hallo und Willkommen zum Rhein-Tal!

Hello and welcome to the Rhine Valley!

You can see that this **valley** is one beautiful place. It is dotted with ancient castles, modern cities, small villages, and rich farmland. The Rhine Valley is one of Europe's most visited areas.

The valley was formed by the Rhine River. The river starts in Switzerland as a small stream and flows roughly north for about 1,300 kilometers (800 miles). It gets wider as it reaches flatter ground. Over time, the moving water eroded the land, creating a wide valley. **Erosion** is the picking up and moving of rocks and soil to a new place.

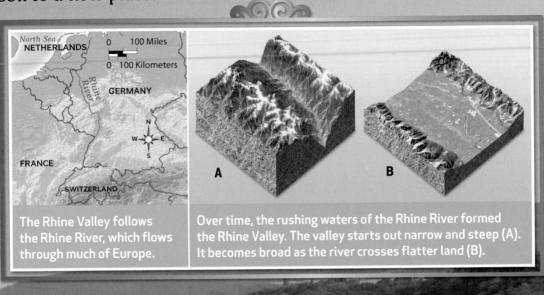

The Rhine Valley follows the Rhine River, which flows through much of Europe.

Over time, the rushing waters of the Rhine River formed the Rhine Valley. The valley starts out narrow and steep (A). It becomes broad as the river crosses flatter land (B).

Living in the Valley

CLIMATE

The landscape of the Rhine Valley changes each season. Most of the valley has warm, humid summers; cool, dry autumns; cold winters; and warm, wet springs.

TRANSPORTATION

The Rhine River has been a major transportation route since the valley was settled. The river links southern and northern Europe. Boats take goods to cities and towns along the river.

WHERE PEOPLE LIVE

The water in the river is an important **natural resource.** People living in the Rhine Valley use the water in their homes, on their farms, and for making products. People settled along the river to use the water supply.

Snow is common in the Rhine Valley. This makes skiing in the surroundings **mountains** possible. Children enjoy playing in the snow, too.

The flat valley floor is a perfect surface for roads and trains. Roads connect cities in the Rhine Valley. High speed trains zip from one place to another.

Centuries ago, castles were built along the Rhine River to protect the land and for easy access to water. Later, villages, towns, and cities developed.

Flowers

The Rhine Valley is perfect for growing flowers. The region has rich, fertile soil. River water is used to water, or irrigate, the land. Rows of tulips and other flowers create bright, colorful fields.

1. PLANTING Tulip bulbs are best planted in the fall before the ground is frozen. They begin to grow underground. In spring, they push to the surface.

2. GROWING Flowers are grown in vast fields. Machines spray water and fertilizer onto the plants. The flowers are harvested just before they bloom.

3. HARVESTING Flowers are harvested and sent to market very quickly. The cut flowers need to be kept in water and in a cool place so they don't dry out.

4. SELLING Cut flowers from the Rhine Valley, especially from the Netherlands, are sold in local markets. They are also sent overseas. The flowers you buy may have come from the Rhine Valley.

Check In How is the Rhine Valley different from where you live?

North China Plain

by Beth Geiger

欢迎华北平原

Welcome to the North China Plain!

You can see far into the distance. There are no big **mountains** or other landforms to spoil the view of the **plain**. But the North China Plain is not all the same. Some areas of the plain include large cities. Other areas are rocky deserts, and still other areas are farmlands.

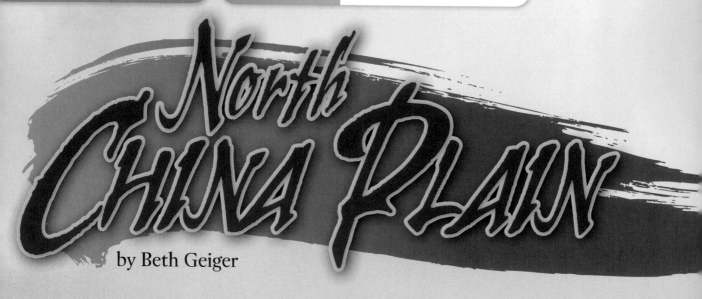

The North China Plain is a vast, flat **landform**. It was made from tiny particles of Earth materials called silt. Over millions of years the nearby rocky highlands were **weathered**, or broken down, until they became silt. The silt **eroded** and was carried down from the highlands by rivers and streams, including the Huang He. When the rivers flooded, they deposited, or dropped, the silt on the land.

The North China Plain is a large flat area in China.

The North China Plain was formed over a long period of time. Rivers deposited layers of silt on Earth's surface like a blanket spread out over the land.

Living on the Plain

CLIMATE

Climate in the North China Plain varies. Some parts are arid, or dry, with little rainfall. Other parts of the North China Plain have floods almost every year.

TRANSPORTATION

The North China Plain is very large. It makes up a large portion of the country of China. Because it is so large, people use different forms of transportation on the plain.

WHERE PEOPLE LIVE

A large part of the world's population lives on or near the North China Plain in the country of China. People live in very different places. Some live in rural villages.

Floods can be dangerous. Dams have been built along the Huang He River to control the flooding. Dams manage the flow of water, but they also block the silt. This means less silt is deposited on the plain.

People living far away from cities often use bicycles, horses, or even camels to travel. High-speed trains and paved roads connect towns and cities.

Others live in major cities. Beijing is a major city on the northern edge of the plain. It is the capital city of China.

Cotton

The silt left behind by flooding has created rich soil for crops. Food crops such as wheat, millet, and corn are grown on the North China Plain. Another important crop is cotton. It is used to make clothes and other goods. China is one of the world's main cotton producers.

1. PLANTING Cotton seeds are planted in rows. The plants grow into cone-shaped plants about 1–2 meters (3–6 feet) tall. They need plenty of water and sunlight to produce cotton. Cotton is ready to harvest in about 200 days after it is planted.

2. HARVESTING
The cotton is ready to be harvested when it looks like small white clouds. After being picked, the cotton is bundled into bales. The cotton bales are taken to factories for processing.

100% Cotton
ONE SIZE
FITS MOST
Made in
China
see reverse
for care

3. PROCESSING
Processing the cotton takes many steps. The cotton fibers are cleaned and spun into cotton yarn. Eventually the cotton is spun into thread.

4. PRODUCING GOODS
Many clothing items are made of cotton. Most goods have a tag attached. The tag states what the item was made from and where. Many goods are made of cotton from the North China Plain.

Check In How is the North China Plain different from where you live?

Discuss

1. Compare the three landforms discussed in this book. How are mountains, valleys, and plains different from each other? How are they similar?

2. What are the different natural resources you read about in this book? Describe how these resources are used.

3. What place described in this book would you most like to visit? Why?

4. What do you still wonder about these places? Where could you go to find more information?